FINISHING LINE PRESS

www.finishinglinepress.com

Making Home

poems by

Elise Marie Toedt

Finishing Line Press
Georgetown, Kentucky

Making Home

ACKNOWLEDGMENTS

I'd like to acknowledge the previous publication of poetry in this collection:

An earlier version of "Pest Control" in *Lumina Literary Journal*
"By Feel" in *Creating a Spiritual Legacy* by Daniel Taylor
"Conversion Therapy" in *Infinite Rust*

The cover art features the work of two artists in Northern Minnesota.
The weavings in the cover art were created by Emily Wick (www.
northwoven.com).
The pottery in the cover art was created by Hannah Palma Laky (www.
hannahpalma.com).

Publisher: Leah Huete de Maines
Editor: Christen Kincaid
Cover Art: Hannah Palma Laky, www.hannahpalma.com and Emily Wick,
www.northwoven.com
Author Photo: Lael Primrose, www.laelprimrose.com
Cover Design: Elizabeth Maines McCleavy

Order online: www.finishinglinepress.com
also available on amazon.com

Author inquiries and mail orders:
Finishing Line Press
PO Box 1626
Georgetown, Kentucky 40324
USA

Contents

A Long Season

Last Fruits

It is winter and the peach tree is dying.
It will not bear fruit in spring, grandpa says.

In April, the snow covering each branch melts
and drips from the tree, mixed with spring's rain.

In May grass grows underneath its boughs.
See, there are no buds, he says.

But as the month rounds to an end
small green heads lift up and push forth.

In June, green fruit grows slow and clings tight.

In July just as the peaches begin
to ripen, flying ants bore through their bodies.

They grow anyhow, soft and pinked, small and sweet.

In August they hold loosely to the tree,
rain and wind battering them down.

We gather those that remain, place them in our basket
and cover them with a red checkered towel.

It is the last season we pick fruit together, peel
the skins, simmer peaches in pots, can for winter.

The day my grandpa dies he reaches out
in front of him, as if picking fruit

and I think of summer, the juice that dribbled
down his chin, sweet for so long

and then how quickly a long season ends.

By Feel

Grandpa calls this time of year the summer doldrums

> He is particularly down today,
> the eye doctor having declared at his check-up
> there is nothing more to be done for him:
> he will soon be blind.

when the hollyhocks lean on each other for support in the heat

> For now, his right eye (with glasses)
> is still good, but not peripherally.
> He cannot read anymore.

and the petunias close their arthritic fists and shrivel up to die.

> I have many memories of him in his armchair
> at midnight: a book in one hand,
> a magnifying glass in the other.

The grass like thin hair, brown and broken—

> He picks the beans by feel now
> and pushes stakes in the middle of his plants
> so he knows where to water.

I think we will all be happy for the rain.

Pest Control

To kill the pests in your garden,
mix 1 part chewing tobacco,

> "I can't believe you make me buy this stuff!" grandma says,
> taking her car keys off the hook and shuffling over to get
> her clutch. "The sales clerk must wonder how I chew snuff
> without pulling out my dentures."

1 part mouthwash,

> "I don't care what he thinks," grandpa returns, wincing in
> her direction. "And make sure you don't buy no brand name
> mouthwash this time. Wasting our money."

1 part dish soap,

> She turns to go, but he continues, "by the way, you've been
> using my soap for your dishes lately, haven't you? That's why
> we run out so fast."

> "It's our soap," she retorts— "and they're our damn dishes."

and pour it into a watering can,
adding water steadily.

> "Well if you want food to put on those dishes, you had better
> stop using my soap." He's really snarling now.

Sprinkle your garden with this mixture regularly.

> "I could buy food just as good as what you grow," she says,
> making her exit.

This is how to keep the bugs away without using pesticides.

> "Ungrateful bitch!" he calls after her.

INFJ

I am his type,
our Meyers Briggs
overlapping on every letter.

When we play Apples
to Apples we always pick
each other's card:

For sadistic, Cold War
not ex-boyfriends
or exterminator or hair dryers.

For neat, refrigerator
not Bill Clinton
or rock n' roll or dining.

His anger a made bed
straightened rug polished
knives everything has its place

the stomp of a foot
an aggravated scream
gestures of our type

I resented him for so long
and myself too.

My Dog Lucky

Eight years old, I dangle Lucky from the second
story landing, his white body trembling

between my fingers, puppy eyes circles of terror.
I recite catechism 43 to him: *what shall be done*

*to the wicked at death? The souls of the wicked
shall be cast into the torments of hell.*

I watch him squirm like I squirm in my nightmares
when God dangles me over the pit of hell.

My stomach turns like I have been dropped— I
hug his shaking body before putting him down.
He skitters away, hiding in my closet.

At night he curls at my feet to sleep.
Sometimes when he dreams his white fur stands
on edge like the tall grass of a frozen field.

When I shake him awake, his eyes
are as round and black as the pit.

What It Tasted Like

I watched my neighbor James in the front yard, holding his sister's face in the snow, her arms flailing like a caught fish.

He let her go when he saw me watching, laughing in my direction. She wiped her eyes with wet gloves, moving quickly towards home through the deep snow.

One bored afternoon the summer before fourth grade, James suggested we play a game. "Let's trick that girl Breanna from down the street. The one that's always playing by herself. We can pretend to invite her to hang out, but really it'll be a trap."

My stomach flipped, a fish glistening up from the water. I listened to him. We tied my rainbow patterned jump rope between two fence posts, put a handful of shaving cream on a patio chair. Poured vinegar into the pitcher of lemonade.

Breanna came over wearing a red dress, her black hair up in a ribbon. She did not trip on the rope. She did sit on the shaving cream and cried when she drank the lemonade, running home, wiping at the white blob on the back of her dress.

"We got her!" James laughed, slapping his knee. "We sure did," I said, taking a sip of lemonade to see what it tasted like. The vinegar burned the back of my throat.

Conversion Therapy

Every emotion we didn't know to name—
a child calling anything blue a lake

everything God,
everything a song

Do everything without
complaining, do
everything without
arguing, that you may
become blameless and pure
children of God.

My mind a room full of
sleep, sweat salty and
breath caught with the door closed,

I think like you taught me.

Never good enough,
afraid behind my ribs
of the hook in hell I'll hang from
for loving the long lashes
of a girl, her voice like a tightrope
where she balances,
her hips meadows I want
to dance in, I am
so good at programming myself

a verse memorized for everything,
names of people to pray for taped
to the shower wall, a song
to cover anger or sadness or fear

I am so good at drowning myself
out. Sin, you say, is the constant struggle
with your carnal being

I see my body roasting over the fire
as you turn the stake,
all the words
that slipped out of my pockets
feeding the flames. I wonder

is love more evil
than obedience?

Did the flames strip me clean
of God? Or is God there,
between my pelvic brim
and floor?

Dear Patriarchy

I do not want to hide behind
any more doors locked between
your lies and my heart which is open
and holds you like the first note
I ever got from a lover or my first poem
come to me like a kiss, firm and sure.

I'm tired of telling myself over and over
you are worthless before I can catch
the words, a kite caught in a devious wind.
I'm tired of tucking myself behind my clavicle,
that triangle container so full my shoulders
round under the weight.

The lidded door between my heart and my lips
is open now and I am not
going to hold you inside anymore.
I don't believe you anymore,
just so you know.

Summer's Fruit

Green and eager, the cucumber plant
grows on top of the tomato plant.

He grasps at her heels, coiling up
her tender body as he spreads

between her limbs, using her just formed
fruits for hand holds. He unfurls

his leaves around her, blocking
her sunlight. His flowers bud

bright yellow as she begins to wither,
her body stretched thin from working

to escape his hold. But he doesn't know
how she buried her seeds, that come spring

she will live again without him,
growing red fruit by the dozens.

Losses

I
On the parched ground
he sells summer's fruits.
Ants squeeze into them
leaving trails of broken
sweetness behind them.

II
The spider was born
full of poison
and when she bit you
she did not know
about the welt

or the itch, the slow
closing of your throat
the tears or the gasping
the dying of breath
and she is very sorry.

III
We heal wounds by laying
the legged bodies of ants
over the open flesh.
When we cut off their heads
they seize up and bind it.

IV
The sea tosses up our losses.
They wash up to shore
polished and white.

Undrinkable

More water my grandma says
so I press a button at her bedside

and her body raises towards me.
I set an ice cube on her tongue.

Talk to me— tell me a story she says
her words like mana left out to dry

my life a wilderness three days past Egypt.

I tell her a story she loves, holding
her hands. If you drink my water

you will never thirst again, Jesus
said to the woman at the well,

her bucket propped against her hip.
I have living water, he told her.

The wind of my voice parts the grey
hair near my grandma's ear.

She coughs, straining forward,
crossing through the river

dry land underfoot, water all around.

Let Them Weep

I salt each sphere of eggplant, leaving them
to rest until each cries out droplets of moisture.
I blot up each tear drawn out. I dip
the spheres in flour, egg, breadcrumb.

I mince fresh garlic, the pungent smell
conjuring memories of my grandma.
I heap it into the cast iron spitting oil.

I add the eggplant, watching them brown,
spatula in hand, vigilant to grandma's
warning— *don't let them shrivel.*

I layer each round slice into a glass Pyrex,
cover them with tomato sauce, layer
them with Parmesan and Romano.

I place the pan in the oven and think
of her last days, of her half smile
when I brought eggplant parmesan.

I wish I could just die she whispered
into my ear as I fed her, sauce
dribbling onto her chin. *Enough is enough.*

Tonight, I remove the dish when the cheese
bubbles brown, at just the right moment.

Making Home

Making Home

I made decisions
and unmade them.

Made homes
and unmade them.

Made love
and unmade love. Change

made me her friend.

I was made resilient
and unmade my resilience.

I met many parts of myself
and made a home for them.

Set Table

Pickled cabbage, beans,
tomatoes and rice
in ceramic bowls
set out for dinner.

Outside the window
a robin perched
on the bird feeder,
squirrels underneath
catching seeds.

Next to the table
a flowering plant,
a kitty curled
on the corner chair.

Love is this now for me—

vegetables are soaked
in vinegar. Plants are watered,
rotated into and out
of the sunlight.

The kitties get wet food
in the mornings, dry food
in the evenings.

You remember
to turn off the stove
when I forget.

Beet Preserves

We tug at the matted leaf heads
of beet plants, thick-skinned
and round. We shake off the garden's
dirt, drop them in our basket.

The kitchen steams with heat
as we scrub the beets, drop them
into boiling water, wait for them
to soften, drain one pot to fill another.

We peel off their warm skin, cut them
into spheres ringed like trees, layer
them into glass jars sealed tight.

Come winter we plunge our fingers
into the beet jars, magenta skin
startling us away from silver sky,
bird shadows and brittle trees.

We taste summer's sun.

Slow Care

I pick the chicken carcass clean of meat,
put it in a tall pot filled with water on the stove.

I add onion peeled and sliced four ways, sage,
tops of carrots and celery, garlic, salt and pepper.

I let it simmer. I add three cups of chicken,
diced carrots and celery, rosemary and thyme.

I make dough for noodles, roll it out,
cut it in strips and drop it into the soup.

I pour the broth in blue ceramic bowls.

My kid and I slurp it up as he chatters
about his day— the Lego tower he built,

his dream at naptime. I think of my grandma

who on Sundays had soup simmering on the stove,
the heat steaming winter's windows.

The smell of garlic and onion promised me
a slow day, naps and reading on the couch.

The most delicious gift my grandma gave me
I give now to my son. *Thank you* I think to her.

I like to think she can hear me.

Labyrinth Winter

The first 50-degree day
after a long winter

so my three-year-old and I go
to the lake. Two pom poms

bounce on either side of his hat
as he pushes himself along
on his balance bike.

"Look at this puddle!" he says,
stopping to stomp in it,

muddy water splashing onto his pants.
I pull my jacket up over my neck,

blocking the wind. He smiles,
says "This is fun, huh?"
Around the lake we go, puddle

after puddle. We stop to watch
geese dunk their heads into the water.

He holds his belly and laughs.
"Why do they do that?" he asks.

Seagulls circle overhead
then land on ice center lake.

It's the end of a labyrinth winter
we twisted and turned though

thinner and thinner ice until
we exit here at spring again,
my child's face delighted by each sign

of season's change: Fat robin in her nest,
burly squirrels he chases beneath the trees
where buds have just begun to form.

It is so simple for him to love his life, I think.
It could be so simple for me to love my life.

Bird Song (or Foreboding Joy)

Green grass and a chickadee sings
small as my five-year old's fist and holding
as much heart, as much glee at today's

rain-drenched flowers, blue hyacinth budding
so fully they are falling over and crabapple trees
every inch a dot of pink. Can I handle

the utter abundance of this season
without my heart freezing in dread?

Can I hold this goodness
tender as a bird song in spring?

Writing Afternoon

I eat a turkey sandwich on sourdough,
crocheted blanket draped over my lap.
Rain falls outside. I do not push myself.

Turning 35 I learned my best lesson
about writing— to let myself be.

To let go of Hemingway drunk,
to take the rocks from my pockets,
step away from the water's edge.

I learned to write while I live—
while I mother, before I go
to work, after I've eaten a good meal.

On a delicious afternoon
I carve out time for myself.

Mattering

My life is small
shoveling snow in winter,
mowing grass in summer.

Clothes go into
the washer and out
dishes into
the sink and out.

Some Buddhists say
this is meditation—
to wash a dish,
to arrange flowers
center table.

When my students
express dread about AI—
we won't matter
we aren't necessary—

I want to hand
them a broom,
ask how they feel
when they sweep.

Is any of life worth living
when it's small,
when anyone or anything
could do the same task?

Maybe it matters
because we are here
And we are doing it.

Green Burial

Let me be a home for new life.

Spread seeds across my tongue
cover them with dirt, pat them
with the flat side of a spade.

Let roots take hold in my throat
fold around my larynx
around pitch and volume

let tender green bodies circle towards
my lips, let my mouth hold them.

Let their tendrils grow anchored
to my teeth, let them thrive.

Come winter let each plant rest
their tired body against my body.

In spring let them sprout new seeds

grow using my bones
bloom over my silence.

In Gratitude

Thank you, God. Thank you to my mentors. Thank you to my writing group and writing friends who read and edited poems in this collection and encouraged me to submit, especially Anna Schick and Abby Boehm-Turner, and the writing group who workshopped with me: Allison Vincent, Michelle Herrin, Matthew Tchepikova-Treon, and Nicole Montana.

Thank you to friends who make a life of critical scholarship and creativity and encourage me to do the same—Emina Bužinkić, Stephanie Johnson, Hannah Palma Laky, Rachel Warner, Anne Nelson, Diana Chandara and so many more. Thank you to my family. Thank you to my kid, Winter, whose curiosity keeps me awake to the mundane and the beautiful. Thank you to the many healers of body and soul who have helped me along my way.

In memory of my Grandma Lottino, who lived on the same plot of land in the south side of Chicago from birth until near her death. On that acre of land, hemmed in on three sides by highways, I learned to pay attention to growing things. I learned contentment comes from perspective, not things.

Elise Marie Toedt is a Minneapolis-based poet, qualitative researcher, and teacher. Toedt received her doctorate in Literacy, Language and Culture in the field of Curriculum and Instruction from the University of Minnesota, Twin Cities. Elise teaches writing and education courses to thoughtful college folx. Elise is interested in our embodied experiences of being human. She explores questions like: How can we engage in practices that counter white supremacist capitalist commitments to hyper-production, fear of rest, and overuse of the earth? How can we cultivate an ethics of care?

Toedt is currently a Senior Lecturer in the Department of Writing Studies at the University of Minnesota.

Her greatest joys are in connecting with others, moving her body in nature, tending a garden, cooking, and in cultivating a life with space for curiosity. She lives in Minneapolis. Follow her creative writing and research at *https://www.elisetoedt.com/*